MASSACHUSETTS

A Turner Educational Services, Inc. book. Based on the Portrait of America television series created by R.E. (Ted) Turner.

Library of Congress Number: 85-11915

Library of Congress Cataloging in Publication Data

Thompson, Kathleen.
  Massachusetts.

  (Portrait of America)
  "A Turner book."
  Summary: Discusses the history, economy, culture, and future of Massachusetts. Also includes a state chronology, pertinent statistics, and maps.
  1. Massachusetts—Juvenile literature. [1. Massachusetts]
I. Title. II. Series: Thompson, Kathleen.
Portrait of America.
F64.3.T48   1985   974.6   85-11915

ISBN 0-8174-435-4   hardcover library binding

ISBN 0-8114-6787-2   softcover binding

Cover Photo: Michael Reagan

4 5 6 7 8 9 0   96 95 94 93 92 91

★ ★ ★ ★ ★
Portrait of AMERICA

MASSACHUSETTS

Kathleen Thompson

Photographs from Portrait of America programs
courtesy of Turner Program Services, Inc.

RAINTREE
STECK-VAUGHN
L I B R A R Y
A Division of Steck-Vaughn Company

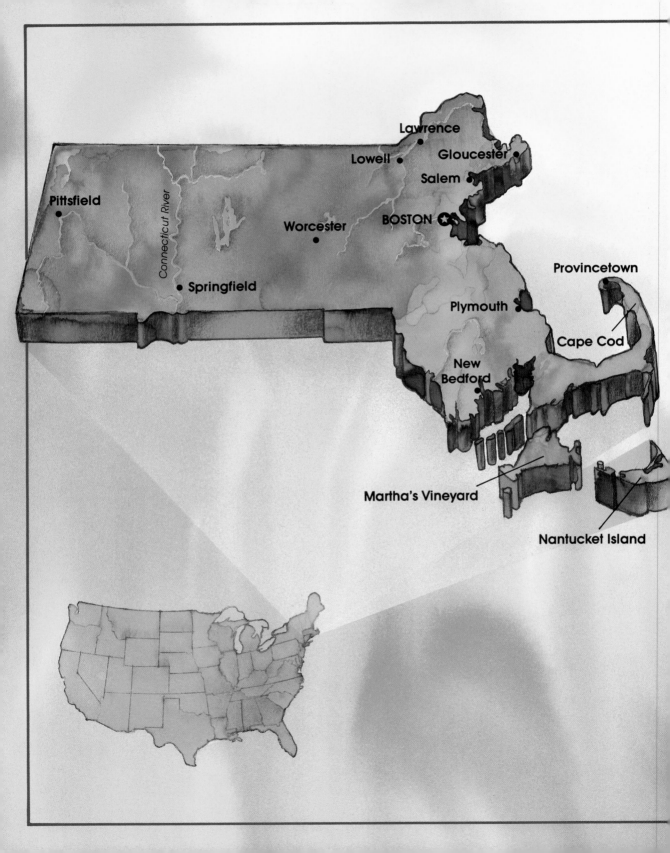

CONTENTS

Introduction

Massachusetts, the Bay State.

"There aren't many places where you would expect to find sixty-three humpbacks (whales) in a few hours. I would say that's pretty exciting."

Massachusetts: history, education, the sea, Boston Brahmins, baked beans, and brains.

"This is the sort of place where someone wins a Nobel Prize and you hear about it—'Oh, him. Oh, I didn't know he was working on anything interesting.'"

"You don't just go out and do something to make money. Or you don't just go out to do something to be busy. Better to stop and think about it."

"For two hundred years, roughly, this was a very homogeneous society here. We were Anglo-Saxons, we were Protestants, we were descended from the Puritans, and the influence of the Protestant Church was very strong. And since then things have changed, and I'm sure they've changed for the better."

Massachusetts is a grown-up state. Its history is long and rich. It has, in its time, been the birthplace of American arts and literature, a center of revolutionary activity, a new home for hundreds of thousands of immigrants, and an educational mecca.

Is there still room in Massachusetts for excitement and new growth?

statue of Paul Revere.

Land of the Pilgrims

The early history of Massachusetts is what people usually think of when they think of American history. This is the land of the Pilgrims and the First Thanksgiving. It wasn't the first place settlers came to on this continent. The Spanish settlement of St. Augustine, Florida, has that honor. It wasn't even the home of the first English settlement. That was Jamestown, Virginia. But Massachusetts is the sentimental favorite.

Before the Pilgrims landed at Plymouth, this part of the country was the home of the Massachusett, Mohican, Nauset, Nipmuc, Pennacook, Pocomtuc, and Wampanoag Indians. At one time, they were at least thirty thousand strong. But early explorers brought European diseases with

A waterfall that looks the same today as it did before the Pilgrims landed.

them. The Indians had no defenses against these new illnesses and they died by the thousands. When the Pilgrims landed, there were only about seven thousand Indians living in the

Below is Plymouth Rock, where the Pilgrims landed in 1620. At the right is Mayflower II, *a reconstruction of how the original ship was thought to have looked.*

area that we now call Massachusetts.

Explorers had been looking over New England for a long time, probably since Leif Eriksson in the year 1000. Captain John Smith, of Virginia, came up to Massachusetts in about 1614. He made a map of the New England area and sent it back to England. Young Prince Charles crossed many of the Indian place names off the map and wrote in English ones, like Plymouth and Cape Ann.

It was at Cape Cod that the Pilgrims landed in 1620 before traveling down to Plymouth.

Most of the 101 passengers on the Mayflower were Separatists. To understand what that means, you have to know that the Church of England was a state church. No other churches were officially allowed in the country. The Separatists were people who wanted their churches to be free from the state church. They came to America to establish a colony where their church would be the church in power—the only church. They did not want freedom of religion in the sense that all people would be allowed to worship as they pleased.

The Pilgrims were not authorized by England to settle in Massachusetts, so they created their own government. They drew up and signed the Mayflower Compact.

When the Pilgrims arrived at Plymouth, it was winter. There was no time to plant and harvest crops. And they did not have enough supplies to feed themselves until a crop could be grown. Half of them died that first winter.

But the Indians of that area, the Wampanoag, helped the new colonists. The Indians taught them about new foods and ways to hunt, fish, plant, and cook in the new land. By the next fall, the colony was in much better shape. People continued to come from England and the colony grew.

After the Pilgrims came the Puritans. The Puritans came for religious reasons, too. They did not want to separate from the Church of England, but they did want to reform it. They were much stricter in their moral beliefs than most of the English people. After they established the Massachusetts Bay Colony, more than a thousand colonists came to Salem and Boston.

Life in the Puritan colonies was lived according to harsh rules laid down by the church and enforced by Governor John Winthrop. Every detail of an individual's life was dictated by the Puritan religion, which outlawed such things as strolling "unreasonably" in the streets, wearing long hair, smoking, and wearing an embroidered cap.

During the 1630s, several

Above is a painting of John Winthrop. Winthrop was the leader of the Puritan colonists, and he founded a settlement near present-day Boston.

Massachusetts Historical Society

other states grew from colonies that were started by people who were banished from Massachusetts. Roger Williams believed, for one thing, that Indians should be paid for their land. He was forced to leave and founded Rhode Island. Thomas Hooker thought that Governor Winthrop's punishments for small sins were too harsh. He founded Connecticut. John Wheelwright questioned Winthrop's ideals and ended up founding New Hampshire.

Three Quakers were sentenced to be hanged for stepping onto the Massachusetts shore. On the gallows, one of them, a woman named Mary Dyer, was told that she could go free if she left the colony. She refused, but she was tied to a horse and forced out. She came back, determined to stand up for what she believed. This time, she was hanged.

Massachusetts was an odd combination of progress and repression. On the one hand, Boston had the first public park in the country, the first public school, the first college, the first bookstore, and the first news-

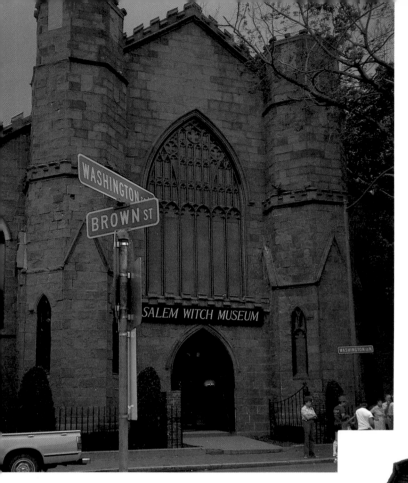

At the left is a witch museum in Salem. Below is the house of a present-day "witch."

Marion Ott Messner

paper—all before 1700. On the other hand, "witches" were executed or put into prison, and Massachusetts shipowners took slaves from Africa and traded them in the West Indies for molasses to bring back to Massachusetts to use in making rum.

By 1700, Massachusetts had 80,000 people. Most of the Indians were gone. Early friendship between Indians and colonists had disappeared as more and

Massachusetts Historical Society

traded goods with countries around the world. But the English wanted their colonies to trade only with them. They passed laws that said that all overseas trade had to be carried on ships owned by the English, and the crews of the ships had to be three-quarters English. These were called the Navigation Acts.

At the left is an engraving by Paul Revere of how he imagined King Philip looked. Below is an engraving of the Boston Tea Party.

more land was stolen from the Indians. The biggest Indian uprising had been led by King Philip, son of the chief who first welcomed the settlers. Between 1675 and 1678, hundreds of Indians and colonists were killed. But there were more colonists, and they had guns. The Indians lost.

There were also troubles with England. The Puritans were business people. They built ships and

The colonists ignored them.

Massachusetts merchants had been making fortunes trading. They took dried fish, corn, salt, and lumber to the West Indies. They brought back cotton, dyes, tobacco, and molasses. They shipped rum made from the molasses to Africa and brought back slaves. They took dried fish to Europe and brought back wine and sugar. These merchants were not about to stop such a profitable trade. All the respectable merchants of Massachusetts became smugglers.

But the British then started collecting taxes, which the colonists could not ignore. The Stamp Act of 1765 led to open rebellion. In 1773, Samuel Adams, Paul Revere, and others dressed themselves as Indians and dumped a whole load of British tea into Boston Harbor to protest a tax on tea.

The British posted more and more soldiers in the colonies. On Saturday night, April 15, 1775, some colonists noticed unusual activity among the troops. They arranged a signal that would tell other colonists when, and if, the troops started to move. In the tower of the North Church, one lantern would mean the British left by land, two meant they left by sea.

At ten o'clock on April 18, Dr. Joseph Warren sent for Revere and told him to ride to the rebel forces to tell them that a group of British soldiers was marching to the dock where boats were waiting for them. Revere sent a friend to put two lanterns in the church steeple and set out

on his horse.

Paul Revere's ride has become a legend. So has the battle fought the next morning, first at Lexington and then at Concord, "the shot heard round the world." The Revolutionary War had begun. It would end eight years later, in 1783.

Portrait of America

In 1788, Massachusetts approved the new Constitution of the United States and became the sixth state. They insisted, however, that a bill of rights should be added to the constitution. The Bill of Rights outlined the specific freedoms of individuals. It was approved in 1791.

In the early years of statehood, Massachusetts continued

At the left is a statue of a minuteman. At the far left is a statue of Paul Revere, and below is the Old North Church, where the lanterns signaled the coming of the British soldiers.

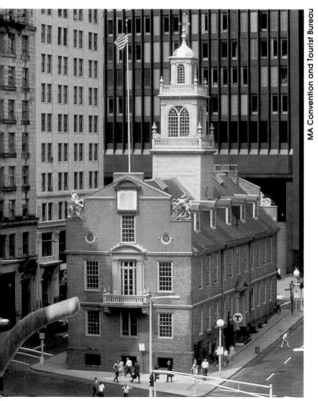

MA Convention and Tourist Bureau

to build ships and do business as traders. When the French and the British went to war again in the early 1800s, shipowners were making large sums of money by using their ships to send supplies to Europe. But President Thomas Jefferson was afraid that the United States would have to go to war, too, if an American ship was attacked by one of the warring countries. So, in 1807, the Embargo Act was passed. American ships were no longer allowed to trade with other countries.

From that time, things changed in Massachusetts. From a state of merchants and traders, Massachusetts was forced to become a state of manufacturers. They had to produce the goods that they had once traded for. Mills were opened to make cloth. Ships were sent south, around the tip of South America, to trade in the West and in the Orient. The trend towards manufacturing increased with the War of 1812.

In the first half of the 1800s, the antislavery movement became strong in Massachusetts. When the Civil War broke out in

1861, Massachusetts sent more than 125,000 men to the Union Army and about 20,000 men to the Navy.

During and after the war, thousands of immigrants poured into Massachusetts. Many of them were Irish. They had left their own country to escape the potato famine. They were poor and hungry. And many of the old-time Yankees resented them. Soon, the Irish faced the most serious discrimination ever seen in this country against whites.

But the Irish had the vote and they knew how to use it. In time, they moved into Massachusetts politics. They still had no wealth, but they had political power. Other ethnic groups who came into Massachusetts followed their example. And there were many of them.

By 1900, 30 percent of Massachusetts's population had been born in another country. By 1920, 67 percent were either foreign-born or had immigrant parents.

The last part of the nineteenth century and the early part of the twentieth century was a period marked by labor troubles in the factories of Massachusetts. But it was also a time of economic growth. When the Great Depression hit the United States, Massachusetts was one of the few states that offered its people unemployment relief until the New Deal program of the federal government could begin.

Two important events occurred between World War I and the Depression. They were the Boston Police strike and the

Sacco-Vanzetti case.

In 1919, the Boston police force went on strike. The commissioner of police had refused to recognize their union. Governor Calvin Coolidge called in the National Guard and ended the strike. His actions made him famous and he was elected vice-president of the United States in 1920.

The Sacco-Vanzetti case began when two men were arrested for murder in connection with the robbery of a shoe factory. The men were Italian-born, and they held a political belief called anarchism. They were convicted of the crime and sentenced to death, but many people felt that their ethnic heritage and their politics had more to do with the conviction than did the crime. Their execution became a rallying point for political groups around the country.

World War II brought a boom in the economy of Massachu-

This is a unit of the National Guard that was sent to end the Boston police strike in 1919.

Courtesy of the Boston Society/Old State House

setts, as it did in most states. But there were changes in the kinds of manufacturing that were important. Shoes and cloth became much less significant. Electronics soared in importance after the war.

In the 1950s and 1960s the

At the left is Senator Edward Brooke. On the right-hand page is a 1946 photograph of (left to right) John, Robert, and Edward Kennedy. Below is the house where the Kennedys grew up.

whole country began to face its racial problems. Massachusetts was no exception. Legislation was passed to prevent segregation in housing. In 1966, Edward Brooke defeated a Boston Yankee to become the first black to win a seat in the U.S. Senate since Reconstruction. When he lost his seat in 1978, it was to the son of Greek immigrants, Paul Tsongas.

Of course, the 1960s were the time of the Kennedys. This Massachusetts family produced John F. Kennedy, president of the United States from 1961 until 1963. And Robert F. Kennedy, United States Attorney General from 1961 to 1964 and New York Senator from 1964 to 1968. And Edward M. Kennedy, United States Senator from Massachusetts since 1962.

Today, Massachusetts remains a place where traditional values face constant challenges from changing times. The state founded by Puritans now has a Catholic majority. The newest wave of "immigrants" consists of young urban professionals who have come to run the largest high tech industry outside the Sun Belt.

And there are no laws against chatting with your friends on the street on Sunday.

Take This Highway ... Please!

"It would have come in at the end of that fence over by the woods and come catty-cornered right across here, right by the end of the henhouse. Seventeen feet in the air. Which wouldn't have been very nice."

Hope Ingersoll laughs as she says it because "not very nice" is such a mild way to put it. For twenty-seven years, she and her farm have been threatened by "progress." To understand what was at stake, you have to understand about the farm.

Hope Ingersoll's mother bought Grazing Fields Farm in Buzzards Bay in 1907. She cleared a small part of the land for a working farm and left the rest of it just the way it was.

"We didn't do any hunting and we tried to preserve everything that was here. There was a great variety of wildlife and lots of birds. People like to go where they can see wildlife, you've got to have a place that's big enough to support wildlife."

The farm is nine hundred acres. A large part of it is still a private nature preserve. The rest of it Hope Ingersoll uses for raising horses. When she was a child, she did farm chores for ten cents an hour. She managed to save two hundred dollars and she bought a pony. She's been a top horse breeder ever since.

That's Grazing Fields Farm. What about progress?

Well, Hope Ingersoll's farm is on Cape Cod. And Cape Cod is one of New England's most popular tourist areas. It's connected to the mainland by a long bridge. On a summer weekend, up to two hundred thousand people may cross that bridge to get to the cape. The new highway is supposed to get rid of some of the traffic jams and allow more people to enjoy Cape Cod more comfortably.

Plans for the highway had it cutting right through the middle of Hope Ingersoll's pasture.

"Well, it was almost unbelievable. Because they had talked about these things for many years past and nothing came of it. But it looked as though they were serious . . . . It was very difficult to find any organization or person that could help to repel this thing that was coming. And we just persisted and persisted and finally came up with some answers."

Hope Ingersoll and various conservation groups fought to save the farm and won. The highway will go around, not across it. As a result of the battle, Massachusetts passed a Wetlands Protection Act that became a model for the rest of the country. And the school children who have visited Grazing Fields Farm for years will keep on coming.

Hope Ingersoll.

Following the Whales

"The imagining I have is that they met on the bank and, as I often say, it's lucky my great-grandfathers were lousy harpooners, because a few of them made it through.... My heritage is in my blood and maybe in my bones and maybe I was destined to do this. And I suppose the whales are tied to the bank in maybe the same way that I am."

Dr. Charles Mayo—known to his friends as "Stormy"—comes from a long line of people who followed the whales. But his great-grandfathers hunted them with harpoons. Dr. Mayo hunts them with a camera. He is a marine biologist. It is his life's work to watch the whales that swim off the Massachusetts shore . . . and to try to understand them.

"What we know of whales is little but that they're large and they're almost extinct. All of us, including myself, make a lot of hypotheses as to where they

travel and perhaps what they do. The fact of it is they spend nearly all their life obscure from us and there's no way we could know them."

But that doesn't stop Stormy. He goes out not in a sailing ship but in a motor boat. His father is at the wheel. His assistant, Carol, is there with binoculars, helping to sight the humpbacks. The boat has radio contact with fishing boats and other craft that give them clues to where the whales might be.

They watch for old friends, whales they've been seeing for years. They watch for new arrivals. They gather information that may help us to understand this mysterious creature of the sea.

"It's important to understand them and hopefully to protect them. It ought to be, somewhere or other, important to the human spirit. Or perhaps . . . the spirit of life on earth that we carry in us."

Dr. Charles (Stormy) Mayo

High Sail to High Tech

They came by sea and lived by the sea. For the early colonists of Massachusetts and for many years of the state's history, the sea was their business. They fished it and they sailed.

Massachusetts shipowners sailed with their precious cargoes to Europe, to Russia, and around Cape Horn. Great fortunes were made. Proud families sent their men to captain their vessels around the world.

The people of Massachusetts were fishers, sailors, and merchants.

Then, in the first half of the 1800s, things began to change. Cotton mills and shoe factories sprang up in the cities and smaller towns. The state of Massachusetts was on

Rockport.

its way to becoming a major manufacturing state.

Today, an amazing 97 percent of the value of goods produced in Massachusetts comes from manufacturing. Agriculture, fishing, and mining divide the other 3 percent almost equally.

The largest area of manufacturing is nonelectric equipment. Massachusetts no longer makes cloth. It makes the machines that make cloth. It makes printing presses, office machinery, and aircraft engines.

Second, and gaining fast, is electric and electronic equipment. The area around Boston is one of the three largest high tech centers in the country. It is second only to the Silicon Valley in California and comparable to Phoenix.

The large number of colleges and universities in the Boston area makes this an ideal place for the high tech industries which need trained people to run the computers and design the programs. And the quality of life in this beautiful, historic city attracts the highly educated employees that are the basis of the high tech industry.

Not all of this area of manufacturing is high tech, of course. Massachusetts factories also make electric appliances and instruments, radio and television sets, and their parts.

The third largest area of manufacturing in Massachusetts comes directly out of the state's sailing past. Boston is a leading producer of measuring devices and scientific instruments.

Massachusetts also makes metal products such as pipes, aluminum windows, and metal tanks. In addition, Boston is a major printing and publishing city.

Massachusetts farmers produce milk, flowers, and cranber-

28

ries, in that order. Dairy products are the biggest source of farm income. But greenhouse and nursery products are a good second. And of course the home of the first Thanksgiving almost has to produce cranberries.

Massachusetts is one of the leading states in commercial fishing. And the quarries of Massachusetts yield up basalt, granite and limestone.

But tourists bring in more than farming, fishing, and mining put together. Millions of tourists come to Massachusetts for the beauty of Cape Cod and the other shore resorts, for the history of Boston, Salem, and the state's other historical cities. They spend about $3 billion in the state each year.

Above is a view of Cape Cod, a major tourist attraction. Below, left, is a cranberry bog; cranberries are the state's third largest agricultural product. Below is the Widmer Library at Harvard University.

A Great Experiment Lives Again

Did you ever go into Lowell, Oh!
*   racket,*
Good Lord what a buzzing it makes,
Like fifty live crabs in a bucket,
And what a darned sight of cotton
*   it takes.*

That verse from an 1849 playbill was talking about the old Lowell, named for Francis Cabot Lowell of Boston. In 1811, he went to England to tour the mills and see the Industrial Revolution close up. What he saw in the lives of the workers he did not like. So, when he and his associates planned a mill town on the Merrimack River, they decided to do things differently.

Their town was in the great tradition of social conscience in this state. The workers, Yankee farmgirls, lived in boarding houses and supported churches, schools, lectures, and even their very own literary magazine. Charles Dickens compared life in Lowell with working class life in England as "Good and Evil."

But the Lowell experiment died, for many reasons. Good working conditions had been given to the workers as a gift, not a right. When they got worse, the workers tried to strike, but there was an almost endless supply of new labor coming in from other countries. The old workers were simply replaced. Finally, in the 1930s, the mills closed.

Today, another man with a

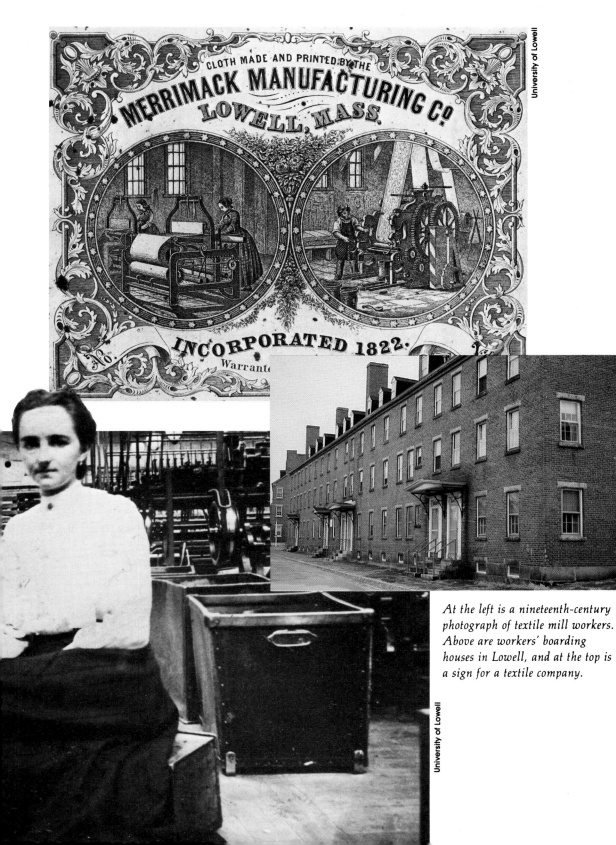

CLOTH MADE AND PRINTED BY THE

MERRIMACK MANUFACTURING Co.
LOWELL, MASS.

INCORPORATED 1822.

Warrant

At the left is a nineteenth-century photograph of textile mill workers. Above are workers' boarding houses in Lowell, and at the top is a sign for a textile company.

vision has come into Lowell. He is Dr. An Wang, founder of Wang Laboratories. His son Fred is one of the top executives in the company.

"The philosophy that my father has

is ... a mixture of the Confucian thought, the American ideals, and the business realities that he's experienced and learned over the years. He very honestly believes that people are the greatest asset. And he feels that you

On the right-hand page, a technician is checking equipment at Wang Laboratories. The inset is Dr. An Wang. At the right is Fred Wang.

Portrait of America

should return more than you actually receive. There are bottom-line goals, profit goals, that need to be balanced out with the betterment of the quality of life and benefits the employees have."

The Wang company provides its employees with a country club, an artists guild, a choral workshop, and a theater group, among other things. The children of workers are cared for at the company's day-care center. The Wangs believe this is not only more humane, but also better business.

"It's much more enjoyable to work in an environment where everybody is very, very enthusiastic. If you keep the people happy, they will do their utmost to really accomplish what needs to be done."

Wang Laboratories Photos

Serious About Life ... and Art

There was a time, in the early years of this country, when people took art very seriously. The job of the writer—the poet or novelist or essayist—was not just to entertain the reader. It was also to try to understand what life was about, how people should behave, and to try to communicate that.

Massachusetts was at the very center of that kind of literary life. In fact, it was in the very center of the artistic life of the new country. To list the important names in the cultural centers of Massachusetts is to give a quick review of early American literature.

In the days of the colonies, there were Anne Bradstreet, Edward Taylor, and Cotton Mather. All were poets whose work reflected the concerns of the Puritan church.

Walden Pond

A little later, Phillis Wheatley was the first black writer published in America. She was born in Africa, brought over as a slave, and educated here in Massachusetts.

The golden age of literature came in the middle part of the 1800s with the Transcendentalists. This group of writers rejected any emphasis on the importance of material things. They believed that the life of the mind and the spirit were what counted and that "The simplest person who in his integrity worships God, becomes God."

There were writers like Ralph Waldo Emerson, Henry David Thoreau, Bronson Alcott, and Margaret Fuller. Around them collected other writers, not always so closely identified with this particular philosophy. They were Henry Wadsworth Longfellow, Nathaniel Hawthorne and Oliver Wendell Holmes, a descendant of Anne Bradstreet. It was the time of William Cullen Bryant, John Greenleaf Whittier and James Russell Lowell. They created American literature. And they all lived in Massachusetts.

Henry Wadsworth Longfellow.

Michael Reagan

Concord Museum

At the left is the one-room cabin that Thoreau built near Walden Pond. The inside of the cabin is shown below.

And at just about the same time, there was a woman in Amherst, Massachusetts, who was writing poems that would not be published until after her death. Today, many people would argue that Emily Dickinson was the greatest poet the United

mings. And a less serious strain was introduced by humorist Robert Benchley and comic playwright S.N. Behrman.

And we can't neglect the painters. The list is astonishing. There was John Singleton Copley and Samuel F.B. Morse, later

At the left is Emily Dickinson. Below is one of Charles Dana Gibson's drawings of his "Gibson Girls."

States ever produced. She wrote with great sensitivity and originality. She also broke through the old forms and traditions of poetry so that, today, her work has a contemporary feeling that can't be found in any other poet of her time with the possible exception of Walt Whitman.

A few years later, Massachusetts produced one of the finest black writers in American literature, W.E.B. Du Bois. He wrote beautifully, and with passion, about his people and the urgent need for justice and equality in this country.

The tradition of fine poetry was carried on by Amy Lowell, Robert Lowell, and E.E. Cum-

known for his work on the tele-
graph. There was John Singer
Sargent; Winslow Homer, the
great painter of the sea; Charles
Dana Gibson, of "Gibson Girl"
fame; James NcNeill Whistler,
known for the *Composition in
White and Black,* better known as
Whistler's Mother; and the famous
Wyeths.

There has always been a rich-
ness and depth to the cultural
life of Massachusetts ... and a
sense that there is more to the
business of life than making a
living.

A Place Where Dreams Come True

"And I say to the children, you know when slave traders came to Africa, they didn't take the worst. They looked for the healthiest, the brightest, the best specimens they could find. You had to have been particularly strong to have survived slavery. Immigrants came looking for opportunity, but your best came. You are the best."

In the Roxbury section of Boston, there is a place that deals in dreams. It began as a small school in 1950. Today, it is the National Center for Afro-American Artists. Here Elma Lewis gives young blacks the chance to believe in themselves.

"It should be normal for people to look at themselves and see beauty. It should be normal to them to look at their music, their dance, their visual imagery, the words they speak, and see that they have offered precious things to the world. ... Duke Ellington at the top of his fame played with the children on the electric pianos. And they have day-to-day contact with these people. It is a privilege to go to that school."

When Elma Lewis made this place, she had a vision. It grew out of her understanding of

This is Elma Lewis against the background of a violin class in her school.

what it was like to be black in America. The way she explains it reflects the history of life in Massachusetts.

"America is not really a place. America is a dream. And peasants all over the world dream the dream and come here looking for the opportunity. When the Irish came, when the Jewish people came, all immigrants, they were white people. Even hostile attitudes were

less hostile. Then, too, they could blend in. But that has not been true for the black citizen because in America, race has been larger than class or effort or any other single thing. The effort, there- fore, must be to reduce the level of racism, so that all people can feel that same dream in coming to America."

Elma Lewis has chosen to work with the young people, with the children. She has chosen to use her vision to make their dreams come true.

"Children are everyone's future."

41

A Future
Rooted in the Past

Massachusetts is a state with so much past that it's sometimes difficult to concentrate on the future. Predictions of great changes and exciting new developments don't come easily. And they shouldn't.

Massachusetts is not a place where things start from scratch much anymore. The new grows out of the old.

It's clear that high tech industries are going to be a big part of Massachusetts's future. But they're in the state because of things that are a solid part of the past and present. These industries are coming to Massachusetts because of the universities and the research facilities and the brain pool that have been building for over three hundred years. They are coming to Massachusetts because their employees want the

The technician above is using a high tech instrument to analyze the boy's brain activity, which will be displayed on a television screen. In the background is a neighborhood produce market.

quality of life and culture which have been developing since the days of the colonies.

The future in Massachusetts is the payoff on investments made long ago. And that's true for the problems as well as the possibilities. Like other places around the country, Massachusetts faces its share of urban unrest. There is a growing need for welfare and social services.

Massachusetts is a state that is densely packed with culture, history, ethnic variety . . . and possibilities.

Important Historical Events in Massachusetts

1602 The English explorer, Bartholomew Gosnold, lands on Cuttyhunk Island and explores the coast of Massachusetts. He names Cape Cod.

1605-
1606 Samuel de Champlain from France maps the New England shoreline.

1614 The English sea captain John Smith sails the coast of Massachusetts and writes the book, *A Description of New England*, which later guides pilgrims to Massachusetts.

1620 The Pilgrims settle at Plymouth.

1621 The Plymouth Pilgrims celebrate the first New England Thanksgiving.

1630 John Winthrop leads a group of Puritans to Massachusetts and founds Boston.

1636 Harvard is the first college founded in the colonies.

1641 Massachusetts sets down the first colonial code of laws, called the Body of Liberties. It provides for political freedom and representative government, but not for religious freedom.

1647 The Massachusetts Bay colony establishes a public education system.

1675-
1678 Massachusetts colonists defeat the Massasoit Indian chief King Philip and his tribe in the struggle known as "King Philip's War."

1691 The Plymouth and Massachusetts Bay colonies are combined.

1692 Nineteen people are hanged in Salem for practicing witchcraft. Sir William Phips becomes Massachusetts' first royal governor.

1704 The *Boston News-Letter*, America's first newspaper, begins publication.

1764 The harsh British tax laws meet resistance from the colonists.

1770 British soldiers kill five colonists, while trying to control an angry mob, in the Boston Massacre.

1773 Angry colonists protest a British tea tax by dumping 340 chests of tea into the Boston Harbor in the Boston Tea Party.

1775 The opening shots of the Revolutionary War are exchanged between American minutemen and British soldiers at Lexington and Concord.

1776 American troops under General George Washington drive the British out of Boston.

1780 Massachusetts adopts its constitution.

1786 Shays' Rebellion is staged in front of the courthouse in Springfield by farmers angry over economic conditions.

1788 Massachusetts passes the U.S. constitution with the stipulation that a bill of rights be added to it. Massachusetts becomes the sixth state of the Union on February 6.

1814 Francis Cabot Lowell builds one of the first factories in the United States at Waltham for the manufacture of textiles.

1820 Maine separates from Massachusetts.

1825 John Quincy Adams of Massachusetts becomes president of the United States.

1831 William Lloyd Garrison of Boston begins publishing his antislavery newspaper *The Liberator*.

1869 The first state board of health in the nation is established in Massachusetts.

1912 Textile workers in Lawrence strike successfully for higher wages and better working conditions.

1919 Governor Calvin Coolidge breaks the Boston police strike by sending in the National Guard. He gains national fame for his action and is later elected vice-president.

1938 A hurricane kills hundreds of people and destroys millions of dollars in property.

1942 The first U.S. jet engines are produced at the General Electric plant at Lynn.

1959 The first U.S. Navy nuclear-powered surface ship is launched at Quincy.

1961 John F. Kennedy of Massachusetts becomes president of the United States.

1966 Edward W. Brooke is the first black to be elected to the U.S. Senate since Reconstruction.

1971 Massachusetts consolidates about 150 of its smaller state agencies into about 10 new departments in an effort to make its state government more efficient.

1976 Massachusetts begins its state lottery.

Massachusetts Almanac

Nickname. The Bay State.

Capital. Boston.

State Bird. Chickadee.

State Flower. Mayflower.

State Tree. American elm.

State Motto. *Ense petit placidam sub libertate quietem* (By the sword we seek peace, but peace only under liberty).

State Song. Hail Massachusetts.

State Abbreviations. Mass. (traditional); MA (postal).

Statehood. February 6, 1788, the sixth state.

Government. Congress: U.S. senators, 2; U.S. representatives, 11. **State Legislature:** senators, 40; representatives, 160. **Counties:** 14.

Area. 8,257 sq. mi. (21,386 sq. km.), 45th in size among the states.

Greatest Distances. north/south, 110 mi. (177 km.); east/west, 190 mi. (306 km.); **Coastline:** 192 mi. (309 km.).

Elevation. Highest: Mount Greylock, 3,491 ft. (1,064 m). **Lowest:** sea level, along the Atlantic Ocean.

Population. 1980 Census: 5,737,037 (0.8% increase over 1970), 11th among the states. **Density:** 695 persons per sq. mi. (268 persons per sq. km.). **Distribution:** 84% urban, 16% rural. **1970 Census:** 5,689,170.

Economy. Agriculture: greenhouse and nursery products, cranberries, apples, vegetables, beef cattle, sheep, hogs and pigs. **Fishing Industry:** cod, flounder, scallops, lobster. **Manufacturing:** electric and nonelectric machinery, electronic equipment, fabricated metal products, food products, chemicals, clothing, textiles, paper products, printed materials. **Mining:** crushed stone, sand and gravel, lime.

Places to Visit

Boston.

Bunker Hill Monument in Boston.

Cape Cod, in southeastern Massachusetts.

Constitution (Old Ironsides) on the Charles River in Boston.

John and Priscilla Alden House in Duxbury.

Old Sturbridge Village in Sturbridge.

Plimoth Plantation in Plymouth.

Walden Pond, near Concord.

Witch House in Salem.

Annual Events

Winter Carnival in Northampton (February).

Patriots' Day in Boston, Concord, and Lexington (third Monday in April).

Boston Symphony Pops Concerts in Boston (May-June).

Bunker Hill Day in Charlestown (June 17).

Berkshire Music Festival, near Lenox (July and August).

Fishermen's Memorial Service in Gloucester (August).

Pilgrim Thanksgiving Day in Plymouth (Thanksgiving Day).

Boston Common Christmas Festival in Boston (November-January).

Massachusetts Counties

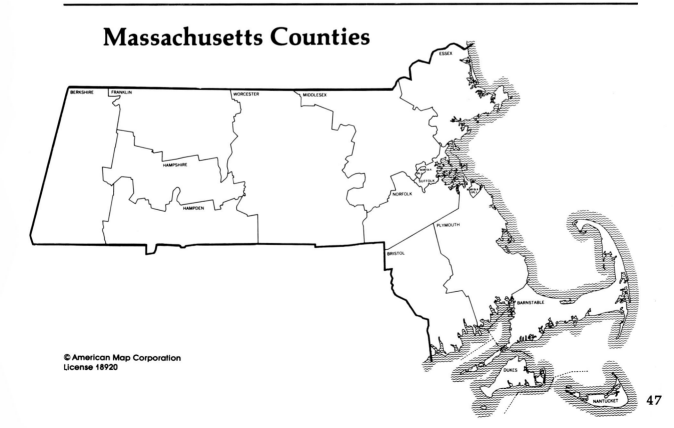

© American Map Corporation
License 18920

INDEX